*giving me
more reasons
to share this
with you!*

FROM

_____

KNOW THAT...

Quotes from Deaf Women
for a Positive Life

—compiled by tina jo breindel

DawnSignPress

san diego, california

Know That: Quotes from Deaf Women for a Positive Life.

Copyright © 1999 by DawnSignPress

Printed exclusively for Deaf Women United, Inc.

Compiled by Tina Jo Breindel

Credit has been given whenever the source for a quote is known. The ideas expressed in this book are not, in all cases, exact quotations, as some have been edited for clarity and brevity. In all cases, the editor has attempted to maintain the original intent. In some cases, material for this book was obtained from secondary sources, primarily print media. While every effort was made to ensure the accuracy of these sources, the accuracy cannot be guaranteed.

ISBN: 1-58121-012-4

10 9 8 7 6 5 4 3 2 1

Printed in Hong Kong

DawnSignPress
6130 Nancy Ridge Drive
San Diego, CA 92121
www.dawnsign.com

KNOW THAT. . .

There never seems to be the right time or place to thank my husband, Joe, and in my haste I often feel I didn't mention my gratitude to him enough. Everyone should be so fortunate to have a mate who faithfully picks them up when they are out of it and enables them to touch the sky. Joe, for the countless times I haven't thanked you enough, let me thank you now.

I also gratefully acknowledge the support of all those who contributed to this book!

*. . . to Deaf women who realize
how special we all are and
how each of us can make a difference!*

INTRODUCTION

In this book **Know That. . .Quotes from Deaf Women for a Positive Life** Deaf women share what we have discovered about life, love, and other good stuff. Quotations were submitted by all Deaf women; women of color, young and old, single and married, straight and lesbian, soccer moms and single mothers, etc. In some instances clarification is made regarding Deaf women who no longer live among us, but who have historical impact and wisdom that lives on. This book illustrates the experiences gained from years of living. Deaf women recognize that there are gender-specific barriers women confront daily, as well as gender-specific strengths. Deaf women often discover that they view themselves as Deaf first, and as women, second. Because of these and other factors, Deaf women have generally been isolated from the insights, knowledge, and tools for change available to more mainstream groups of women sharing with each other. This book is a beginning, addressing the need to pull together.

We do our personal best, reach higher than we thought possible, share visions and resources needed to empower other Deaf women, work together for diversity and greater success of Deaf women, and contribute to life each day in some way.

DW cannot succeed without U!

Some of the proceeds of this book are donated to Deaf Women United, Inc. (DWU), a non-profit organization of, by, and for Deaf women. Its *primary purpose is to promote and educate Deaf women in all walks of life—Deaf culture, politics, employment, and education—and to provide opportunities for social activities and networking. DWU, Inc. was founded in 1985 and sponsors a national conference every two years that focuses on current issues and updated information for its participants.*

We think you will become fond of many of the personalities—the great minds—of the Deaf women who express themselves in this book. You will come back again and again for a treasury of quotes from Deaf women that encourage, inspire, or give a good laugh. Being involved is one of the most important gifts to give to ourselves. Give yourself the gift of sharing this book with your friends.

—tina jo breindel

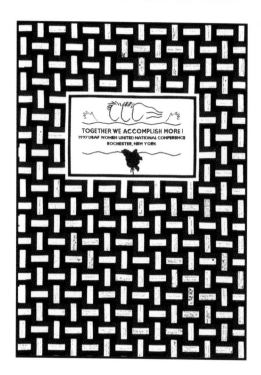

TOGETHER WE ACCOMPLISH MORE!
1997 DEAF WOMEN UNITED NATIONAL CONFERENCE
ROCHESTER, NEW YORK

KNOW THAT. . .

The Deaf Women's Signature Quilt was signed by 356 Deaf Women for the Sixth DWU conference held in New York in 1997. It represents hundreds of women who make our Deaf culture rich and unique. Truly, we can show what our conference theme implied, "Together We Accomplish More!"

—sally a. taylor

KNOW THAT. . .

Before my daughter was born,

I sought to impress others.

Now I only want to

impress her. After all, I am

her first role model.

—damara paris

KNOW THAT. . .

A woman's pen can be mightier than any sword. Let's keep on polishing our pens!

—nancy e. kensicki

KNOW THAT. . .

Care to dare
and dare to care.

—roz rosen

KNOW THAT. . .

Because of our diverse
backgrounds and our gender,
society puts us through
countless struggles in
all walks of life.
Our goal as Deaf women
is to be the best we can be,
learn from experiences life
provides us, and be role models
for the next generation.

—karen frohman

KNOW THAT. . .

Live

and

lead

with love.

—sharon h. carter

KNOW THAT. . .

By learning,
you will teach;
by teaching,
you will learn.

—arlene blumenthal kelly

KNOW THAT. . .

We have two choices. . .

*to follow the carrot,
or be the carrot.*

—sharon kay wood

KNOW THAT. . .

don't sit back
and dream about it.

do something about it!

—dorothy "dot" miles

KNOW THAT. . .

**You are
the artist
of your life.
Paint that picture!**

—debbie sonnenstrahl

*I'm proud
to be known
as one of the
Deaf women.*

—isabelle r. calvacca

KNOW THAT. . .

*LOVING someone
is a wondrous thing.*

*KNOWING that you do
is a blessing.*

—mary anne pugin

KNOW THAT. . .

> To succeed in life, it takes
> traveling different roads
> *(short, long, smooth or rough)*

To reach your destination,
> you will get there one way
> or another.

—marsha wetzel

KNOW THAT. . .

Obstacles
are meant to be removed.

Do not give up
until you have removed
whatever obstacles
stand in your way.

—carolyn mccaskill-emerson

KNOW THAT. . .

A good leader guides

others toward discovery

of their own special talents.

—judy mounty

KNOW THAT. . .

We must prepare
ourselves for
tomorrow's
challenges
and opportunities
because there will be
so much ahead of us!

—maida marinaro

KNOW THAT. . .

If you think you can do it,
do it.

Don't let anyone or
anything stop you
from doing it because
you know you can.

—thelma i. schroeder

KNOW THAT. . .

*To stick to your
convictions in the
face of adversity is
often a very lonely
journey. It is also
one of the most
courageous things
you can ever do.*

—marilyn j. smith

KNOW THAT. . .

Feminism is
the radical notion
that WOMEN
are people.

—mj bienvenu

KNOW THAT. . .

*My mother is the
greatest woman of all,
and I am becoming
my mother.*

—robin m. taylor

KNOW THAT. . .

*Let's enhance the path
to a brighter, barrier-free
future for young
Deaf women
so that they
can leap to
new heights!*

—vicki t. hurwitz

KNOW THAT. . .

Believe in yourself
and then
you can
make a difference
for life.

—linda k. nelson

KNOW THAT. . .

Keep your mind open,
trust in yourself and let go.

> You will find your way out
> of the maze and be amazed
> at the mystery of the puzzle
> being solved.

Life is evolving before
your eyes and your heart.

—toby silver

KNOW THAT. . .

Life is precious.
Make the best of it!

—lori k. bonheyo

KNOW THAT. . .

THE THINGS WE TELL
OURSELVES BECOME REALITY:

Say women and men are equals.
Think women are equal to men.

—petra m. rose

KNOW THAT. . .

What I am looking for

is a blessing that is

not in disguise.

—kitty o'neil collins
stunt woman

KNOW THAT. . .

*Live life to the fullest
and treat every moment
as an empowering one!*

—katherine jankowski

KNOW THAT. . .

The hands in the heart

encourage you to feel

welcome and to become

open about everything

around you.

—sandy mclennon

KNOW THAT. . .

If I had one message to give

employers, it would be to look

at the person before them and

see what they have to offer,

not what is missing.

—karen l. meyer
first deaf correspondent

KNOW THAT...

*Don't get discouraged
when you receive a "No."*

*You must sell yourself and show
that a Deaf woman is capable
of achieving anything.*

—senda senaissa

KNOW THAT. . .

A little sign
of encouragement
and inspiration
keeps one going:

Thumbs Up!

—denise anderson

KNOW THAT. . .

*Don't worry
about meeting
the expectations
of society.*

*Be yourself
and do what you do best!*

—jo bienvenu

Do not dwell too much on the past, focus on the present, and the future will take care of itself.

—genie gertz

KNOW THAT. . .

There is room

in the world

for Deaf women leaders

and Deaf heroines

aspiring to the heights.

—edna adler

KNOW THAT. . .

Laughter has a magical way of shortening the distance between people.

Deaf women who laugh together stand the best chance of understanding each other.

—robin ching

KNOW THAT. . .

Every season of a

Deaf woman's life

reveals a beauty

all its own!

—tina jo breindel

KNOW THAT. . .

*I don't think
Deaf women realize
the extent to which
they are needed.
There are many contributions
they could make, especially
older Deaf women.*

—julia burg mayes

KNOW THAT. . .

I would never want to trade our nine Deaf children for hearing children. They laughed, talked, played, and got mad just like any other children.

—esther docktor frelich

KNOW THAT. . .

Savor kindness

today

because cruelty

is always possible

later on.

—ellen roth

KNOW THAT. . .

WE NEED to shape our own
future, identify and rally support
from our fellow sisters for visions,
hopes, plans, and goals that we as
Deaf women embrace individually
and collectively, and to articulate
values which we hold dear.

—sharon heiydt carter

KNOW THAT. . .

Go after your dream

with your head

and heart.

—roz rosen

KNOW THAT. . .

Women should be free as
the air to learn what
she will be and to devote
her life to whatever vocation
seems good to her.

—agatha tiegel hanson
first gallaudet female graduate

KNOW THAT. . .

Without a struggle,
there is no progress.

—ruth kronick

KNOW THAT. . .

In the tradition of women, independence is a true blessing in life for any Deaf woman.

—dolores goldman

KNOW THAT. . .

Sarah, my daughter,

has taught me so much about…

communication between

two people.

—marlee matlin

KNOW THAT. . .

Washing one's hands
of the conflict
between powerful
and powerless
means to side
with the powerful,
not to be neutral.

—marie philip

Before my son
Jayson was born
I thought of myself,
now I think of us.

—coreen harting

KNOW THAT. . .

I see flowers sway to the mus
It's as if the flowers could hea
My ears may be different bi
And, I can't imagine it mo

I see birds chirpin
As if they know wheth.
My voice may not be perfect bi
are all that is needed t
I am Deaf and I have been ab.

've created in my mind. . .
 my music written in the wind.
 music alone is so beautiful
 powerful if I could hear.

 ove tunes. . .
 'm in love or not.
 facial expressions and words
 nderstand beauty and hatred.
 o create the music inside me.

—shana gibbs

KNOW THAT. . .

*i*t is no fun being
who you are
not.

—mj beinvenu

50

KNOW THAT. . .

My mother was telling me—
With four children…
            one needed glasses,
            another needed braces
and two more needed hearing aids.
            We all have something
      to deal with and you all can!"

That gave me the core strength
      to deal with adversity.

—mary beth barber mothersell

KNOW THAT. . .

Change the Environment,
Not Yourself.

—edna johnston

KNOW THAT. . .

IF AT FIRST
you don't succeed. . .stop!
You may be going
about it the wrong way.
Step back, analyze the situation,
and try again differently.

—carol a. padden

KNOW THAT. . .

What is good for

your mind,

body,

and soul. . .

giving your time

to others!

—karen sheffer-tucker

KNOW THAT. . .

Life has
plenty
of
potholes,
but we
must
drive
past
with
good tires.

—suzanne l. stecker

KNOW THAT...

My deafness is something
special and I treasure it, and
I don't want it taken away.

I want to stay as I am.

Sometimes my deafness
has even helped me.

—evelyn glennie
solo percussionist

KNOW THAT. . .

the best stress reliever is to get involved in a great hobby, like rubber stamping.

You will discover a world of art where your imagination goes in any way as you like.

—teresa t. murbach

KNOW THAT. . .

*A Deaf woman's
soul, mind, and body
should be her own to
mold and cultivate—
one way to do it
is by starting to
believe in
yourself.*

—cinnie macdougall

KNOW THAT. . .

Every now and then

when we are in

an impossible situation

we seem to make things

possible every time.

—toby silver

KNOW THAT. . .

*Ask not what
the Deaf community
can do for you,
but ask what you can do
for the Deaf community!*

—debby sampson

KNOW THAT. . .

*Deaf people do have
five senses just like
hearing people.*

*We have sense of sight,
taste, smell, touch,
and humor.*

—edna johnston

KNOW THAT. . .

Life is wondrous—

make life enjoyable

educational and

beneficial.

—josephine bergner

KNOW THAT. . .

Life is

boundless

in its possibilities.

—suzanne singleton

KNOW THAT. . .

My friends have made the story of my life. In a thousand ways they have turned my limitations into beautiful privileges and enabled me to walk serene and happy.

—helen keller

KNOW THAT. . .

I've got something for the girls. . .

and all America, and all the world,

and we are going to start it tonight.

—juliette gordon low,
founder of the Girl Scouts of America

KNOW THAT. . .

*Intelligent Deaf women
talk about ideas—*

Average women talk about things—

Small people talk
about other people!

—lynn jacobowitz

KNOW THAT. . .

Being self-sufficient

will bring you

greater rewards.

—rebecca j. aranda

KNOW THAT. . .

Carrying a lot of baggage is not going to help you, but if you only keep them light in your mind to help you remember and improve future situations.

—monique holt

KNOW THAT. . .

If you can look back

on your life without regrets,

you have one of life's

precious gifts!

—majoriebell stakley holcomb

KNOW THAT. . .

The contributions
we make to other
Deaf women. . .

will come back to reward us.

—donna dimarco

KNOW THAT. . .

I not only gave birth
to my son, I was born
into a powerful
womanhood.

—robin m. taylor

KNOW THAT. . .

Every non-profit organization relies on the dedication of their volunteers. We often take their time and work for granted. Be sure to give them the praise they deserve.

—teresa t. murbach

KNOW THAT. . .

*Living each day as it comes
is the power and strength. . .*

*of living your life the way
you are–"Womyn-Deaf"*

—vikee waltrip

KNOW THAT. . .

What is hope?
It is to aim the good thing
with moderate wish and smile,
but it is not a violent emotion.

—alice cogswell,
first female gallaudet student

KNOW THAT. . .

*The most important
characteristic a Deaf woman
could have is integrity;
without integrity,
all other values and
accomplishments
are meaningless.*

—damara paris

KNOW THAT. . .

*Having ears
is not just
hearing.*

*With eyes,
seeing is
believing!*

—barbara g. goldman

KNOW THAT. . .

Diversity is a fact of life.
People from different cultures
live beside one another.
We must share our knowledge,
thoughts and feelings
so that we, as members
of the human race,
can understand and
appreciate one another.

—shirley allen

KNOW THAT. . .

Deaf women are no longer
perceived as having the same
old predictable careers.

They now have challenging
juggling acts to perform
and oftentimes outperform
not only men, but themselves!

—jackie roth

KNOW THAT. . .

D o we just value beauty, intelligence, and success? We should not overlook the moral values that make a person wholesome; compassion, giving, honesty, and love.

—elaine anderson

KNOW THAT. . .

*I'm perfect
in my imperfection.*

—marla hatrak

KNOW THAT. . .

When we realize how we have accepted outside definitions of ourselves, we begin to create our definitions, focusing on our strengths as Deaf women.

Within our language and our culture, we begin to focus on our development as women.

—barbara kannapell

KNOW THAT. . .

*If it weren't
for our moms,
we wouldn't be here!*

—beverly buchanan

KNOW THAT...

Communicate, learn, share,
and connect at the library.
No matter where people
–deaf and hearing–
live, work, go to school, or travel...

Libraries Can Save Lives.

—alice l. hagemeyer
friends of libraries for deaf action (FOLDA)

KNOW THAT. . .

*A person without art
is like life without the sun!*

*Nothing would be animated
where all the beauty would be
in the color of gray.*

—julianna fjeld

KNOW THAT. . .

*Be
all
you
can
be!*

—barbara j. keene

KNOW THAT. . .

The ingredients for success. . .
are a vision, hard work,
tears, support from true friends,
faith in God, perseverance,
patience, and hope.

—karen frohman

KNOW THAT. . .

Dream all you want
with your eyes
OPEN.

—tina jo breindel
editor of this very book